Questron®

GW01417897

Compendium of Games

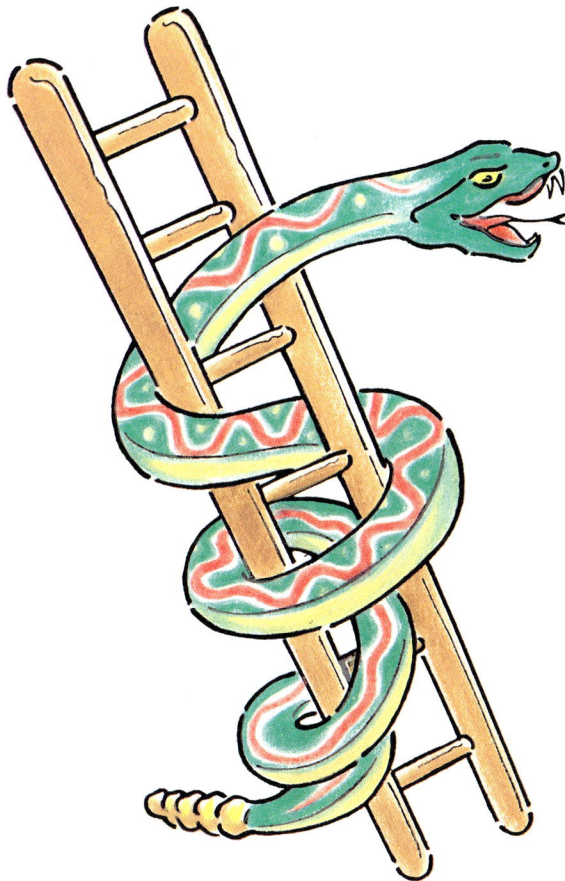

SERIF GAMES LIMITED

SERIF HOUSE, HADLEIGH ROAD, IPSWICH, SUFFOLK, IP2 0EE

Questron

The fun way to bring learning to life

This book is part of the **Questron** system, which offers children a unique aid to learning and endless hours of challenging entertainment.

The **Questron** Electronic Answer Wand uses a microchip to sense correct and incorrect answers with "right" or "wrong" sounds and lights. Victory sounds and lights reward the user when particular sets of questions or games are completed. Powered by an alkaline battery, which is activated only when the wand is pressed on a page, **Questron** should have an exceptionally long life. The **Questron** Electronic Answer Wand can be used with any book in the **Questron** series.

Questron notes to parents . . .

With **Questron**, right or wrong answers are indicated instantly and can be tried over and over again to reinforce learning and improve skills. Children need not be restricted to the books designated for their age group, as interests and rates of development vary widely. Also, within many of the books, certain pages are designed for the older end of the age group and will provide a stimulating challenge to younger children.

Many activities are designed at different levels. For example, the child can select an answer by recognizing a letter or by reading an entire word. The activities for pre-readers and early readers are intended to be used with parental assistance. Interaction with parents or older children will stimulate the learning experience.

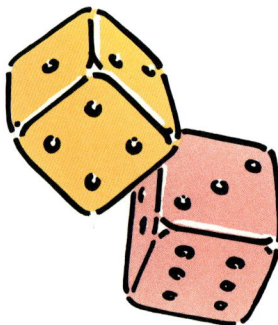

Design	Millions Design
Illustrators	Jim Hanson and Stefan Morris

Printed in Great Britain by BPCC Paulton Books Limited

How to start
Questron®

Hold **Questron**
at this angle and press the
activator button firmly on the page.

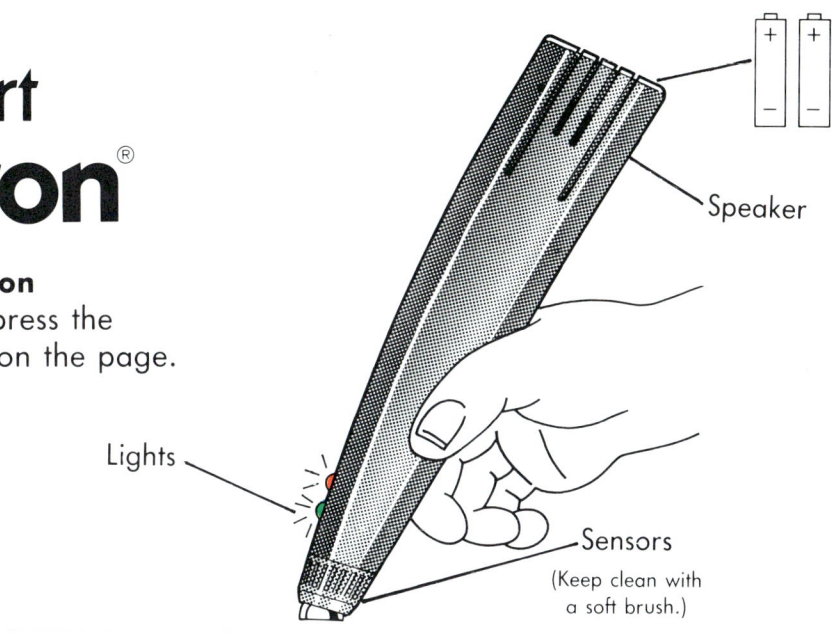

Questron
use two 1.5 volt
alkaline batteries.
Size AAA

Speaker

Lights

Sensors
(Keep clean with
a soft brush.)

How to use
Questron®

Press

Press **Questron** firmly on
the shape below, then lift it off.

Track

Press **Questron** down on "Start" and keep it
pressed down as you move to "Finish".

Start

Finish

Right and wrong with
Questron®

Press **Questron**
on the square.

Press **Questron**
on the triangle.

Press **Questron**
on the circle.

See the green light and
hear the sound. This
green light and sound
say "You are correct".

The red light and sound
say "Try again". Lift
Questron off the page and
wait for the sound to stop.

Hear the victory sound.
Don't be dazzled
by the flashing lights.
You deserve them.

Study this list of words. Some of them cannot be made from the letters above. Use Questron to spot the words that *can* be made from 'compendium'.

upon

medium

mice

poem

model

mime

piece

dome

pond

commend

pump

mode

nice

dope

nine

dune

open

pint

NDIUM

pine	rope
cope	dupe
nude	mope
camp	code
dice	moment
command	dump
deuce	spend
dine	moped
mend	cupid
mine	condemn

Bingo

Study the numbers on the discs. Now look at the cards... Can you find the only one which has all of these numbers on it? Use Questron to check by pressing it on the card of your choice.

The discs show: 36, 72, 15, 49, 28, 89

Blue card (top left):

7	22			55	72	89
		28	40			94
16	36	49	66	87		

Pink/grey card (top right):

1		36	49	66	
7	22	40		72	89
15	28		55		94

Green card (right):

	22	36	49		87
7			55	66	89
15	23	40		72	94

Yellow card (middle left):

7	22		49	72	
15		36	55		94
	28	40	66	87	99

Olive card (middle right):

8	22	40	55	72	
	28		66	87	89
15	36	49			94

Pink card (bottom left):

	22	36	55	72	89
7	28	40	66		
15		49		87	94

Blue card (bottom right):

	20		49	72	
7		33	55	87	89
15	28	36	66		94

6

94
87
22
7
40
55
1 49 66 89
22 36 55 72
7 28 40 87 94
7 36 66 89
22 40 49 72 94
15 28 55 81
22 36 55 72
7 40 87 89
15 28 46 66 94
7 40 72 89
15 22 49 55 94
17 36 66 87
23 55 72 89
7 28 40 87
15 36 49 66 94
7 36 55 89
15 22 66 72 94
28 49 67 87
7 40 55 72 89
15 28 49 77 94
22 36 66

What is the total of the top line of numbers on the correct card?

362 | 258 | 315 | 274 | 212

The Questron Gold Cup

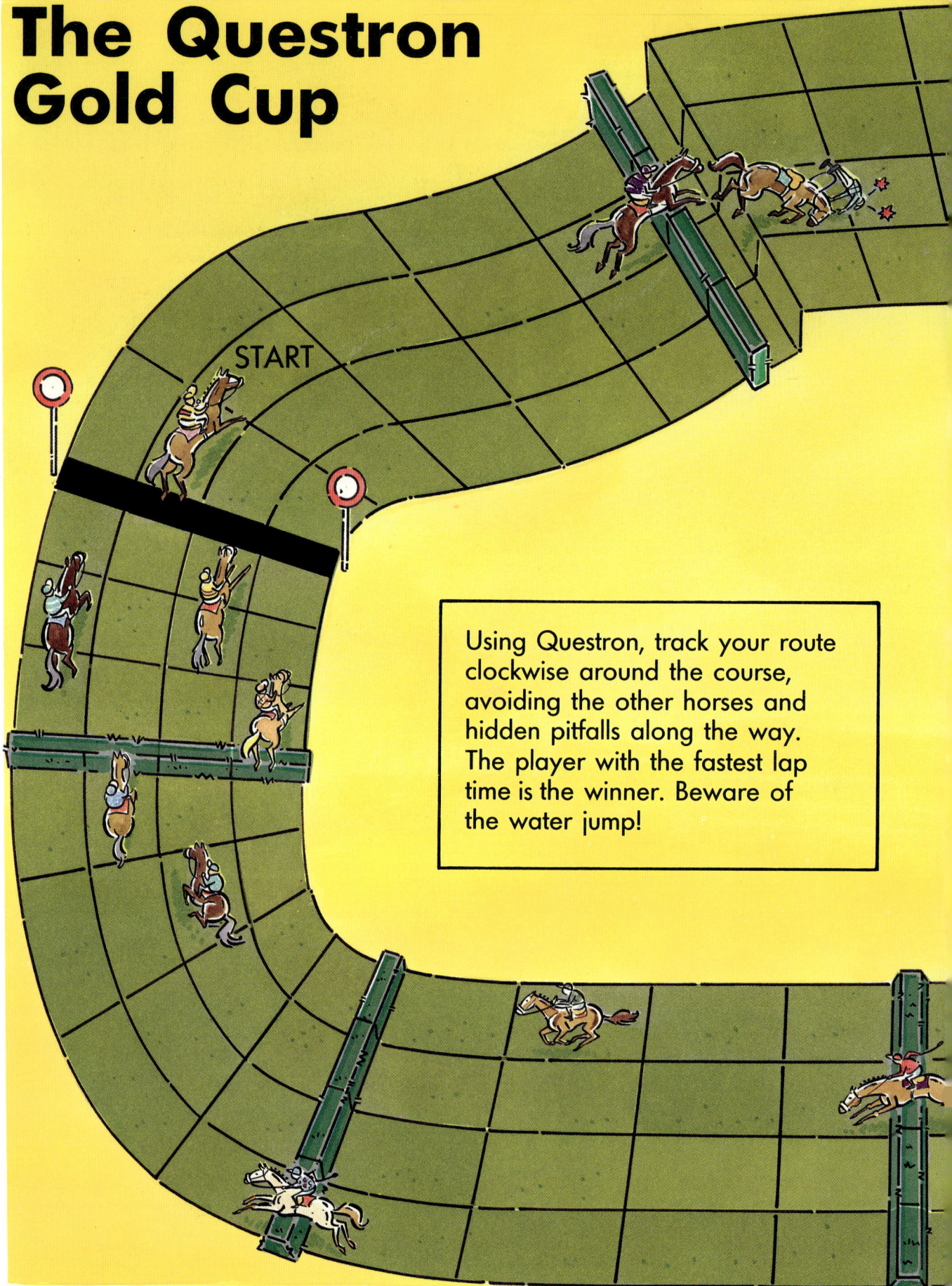

START

Using Questron, track your route clockwise around the course, avoiding the other horses and hidden pitfalls along the way. The player with the fastest lap time is the winner. Beware of the water jump!

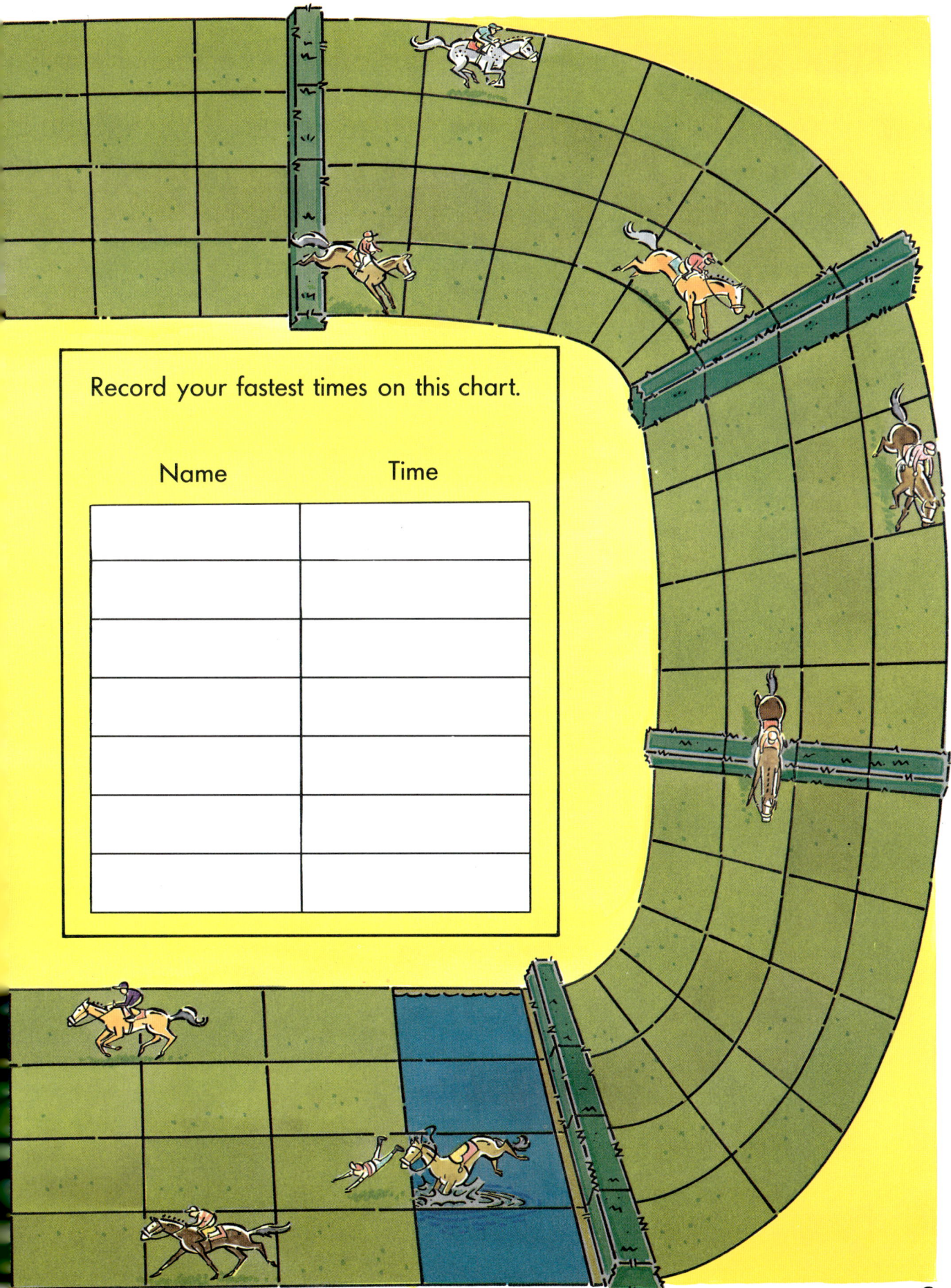

Record your fastest times on this chart.

Name	Time

Slalom

This is a test of your dexterity and memory. Time yourselves on each of the slopes; red for beginners, green and blue for experienced players. The idea of the game is to get the best time (out of three goes) on each of the three slopes.

START

Ghost Hunt

How successful a Ghost Hunter are you? Starting at the main archway, track Questron along the winding, hidden routes to the ghosts. See how many ghosts you can reach before you come off the secret route.

START

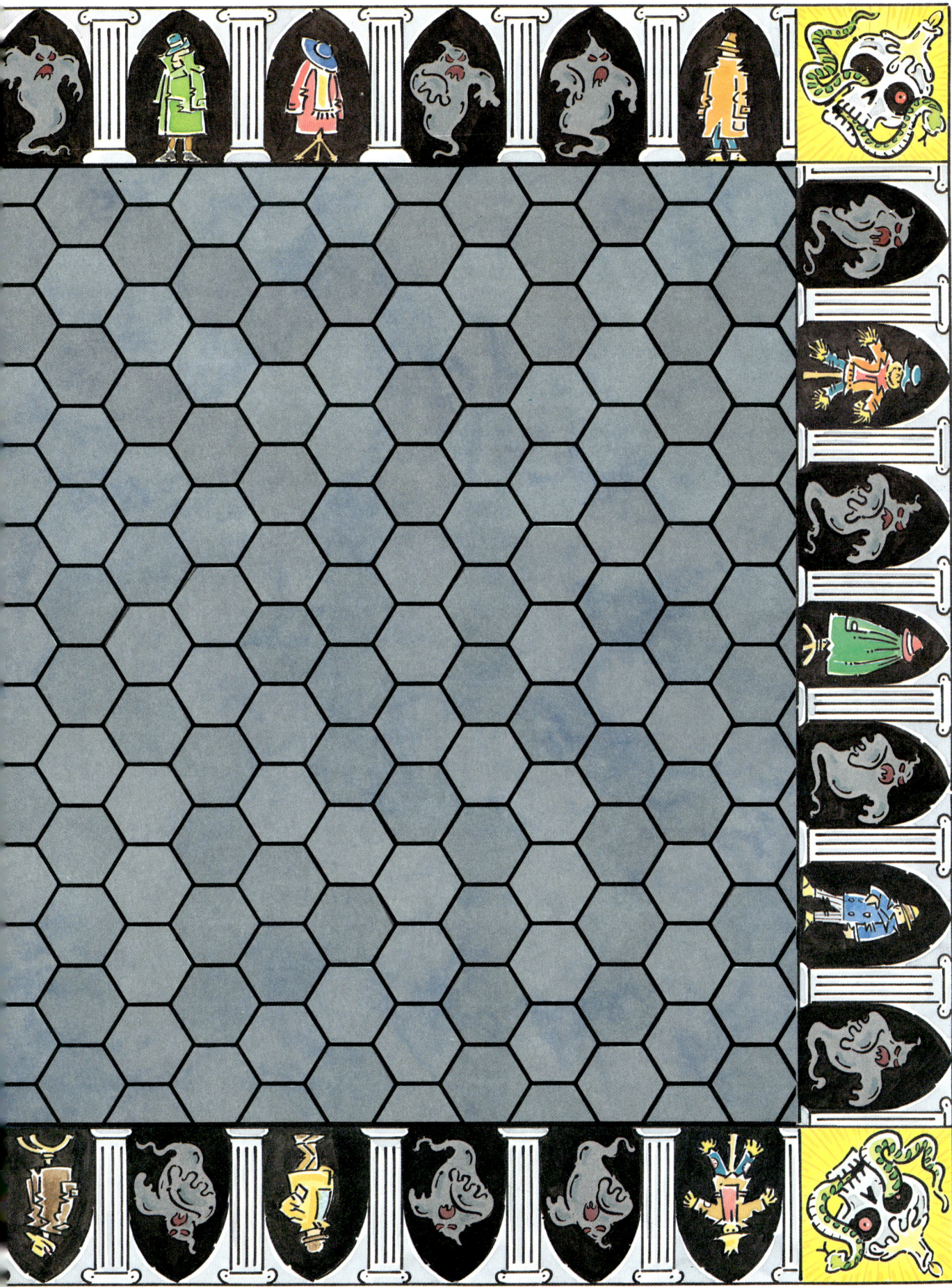

Spot the Ball

Use Questron to find the position of the invisible football hidden somewhere in the picture. How many attempts does it take you to find it?

Snakes & Ladders

Starting in the lower left-hand corner square, work your way to the top left-hand corner. You cannot cross over snakes but you can cross over ladders. There are also some squares which are hidden pitfalls. Each time you come across one of these, or if you accidentally touch a snake, you must go back to the beginning.

How long does it take you to reach the end?

If there are two or more players, each time one has to go back to the beginning, the next player has a go, and so on.

The winner is the first one to reach the finish.

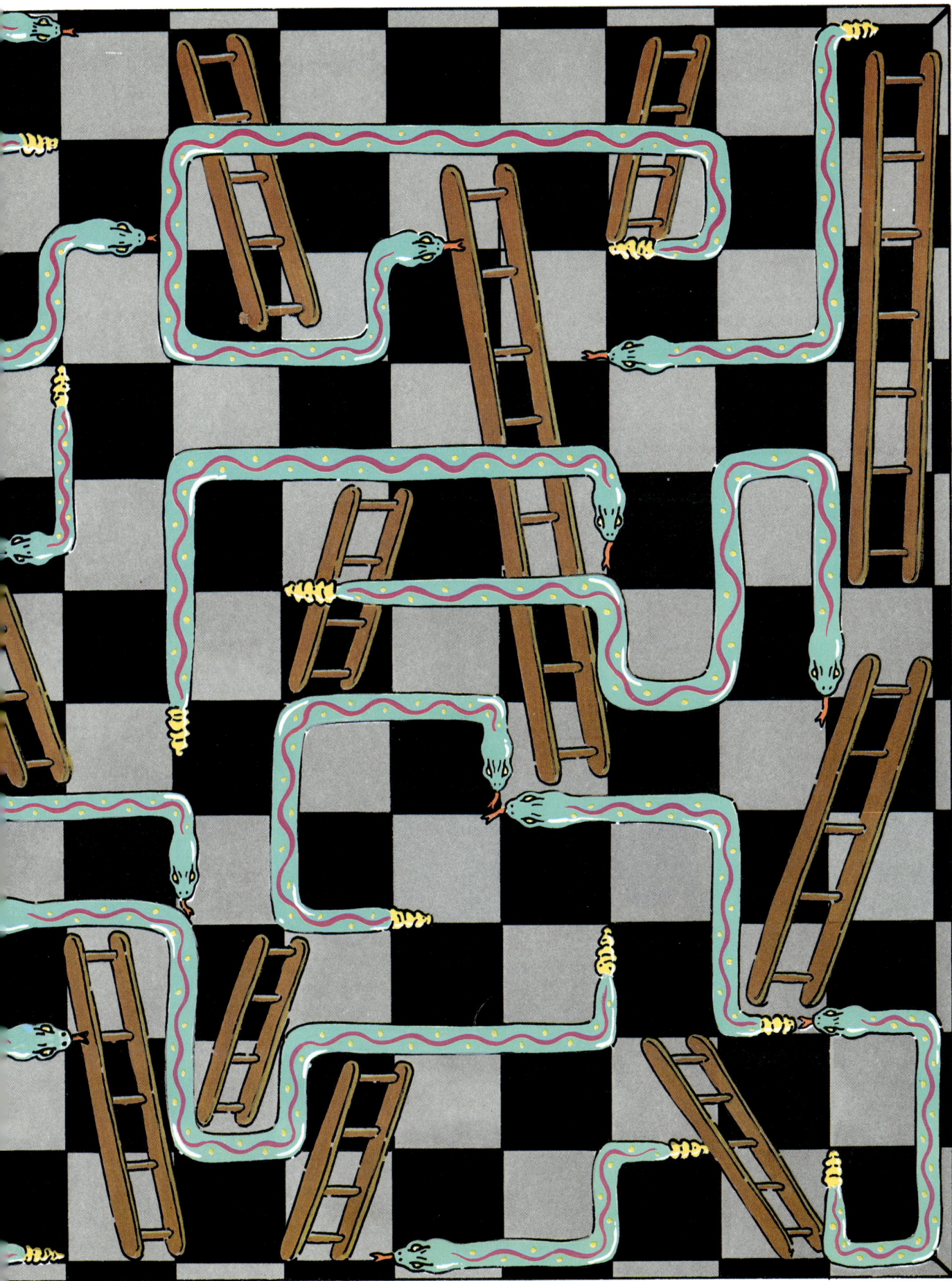

Chinese Checkers

Start at any black spot and track Questron across the board avoiding contact with any of the coloured dots. (If you touch one you will have to go back to where you started.)

Visit each of the other 11 black dots counting as you go, before returning to where you began.

This is a game of dexterity. It looks easier than it is. Especially if you try and do it quickly.

Now study the triangles opposite. One of them is not part of the checkers board on this page.

Use Questron to spot it.

Hex Game

Use Questron to track a route through the Hex maze, avoiding black hexes and red dots. The object is to visit as many green dots as you can on the way. Can you work out a course, visiting 8 green dots, without retracing your steps?

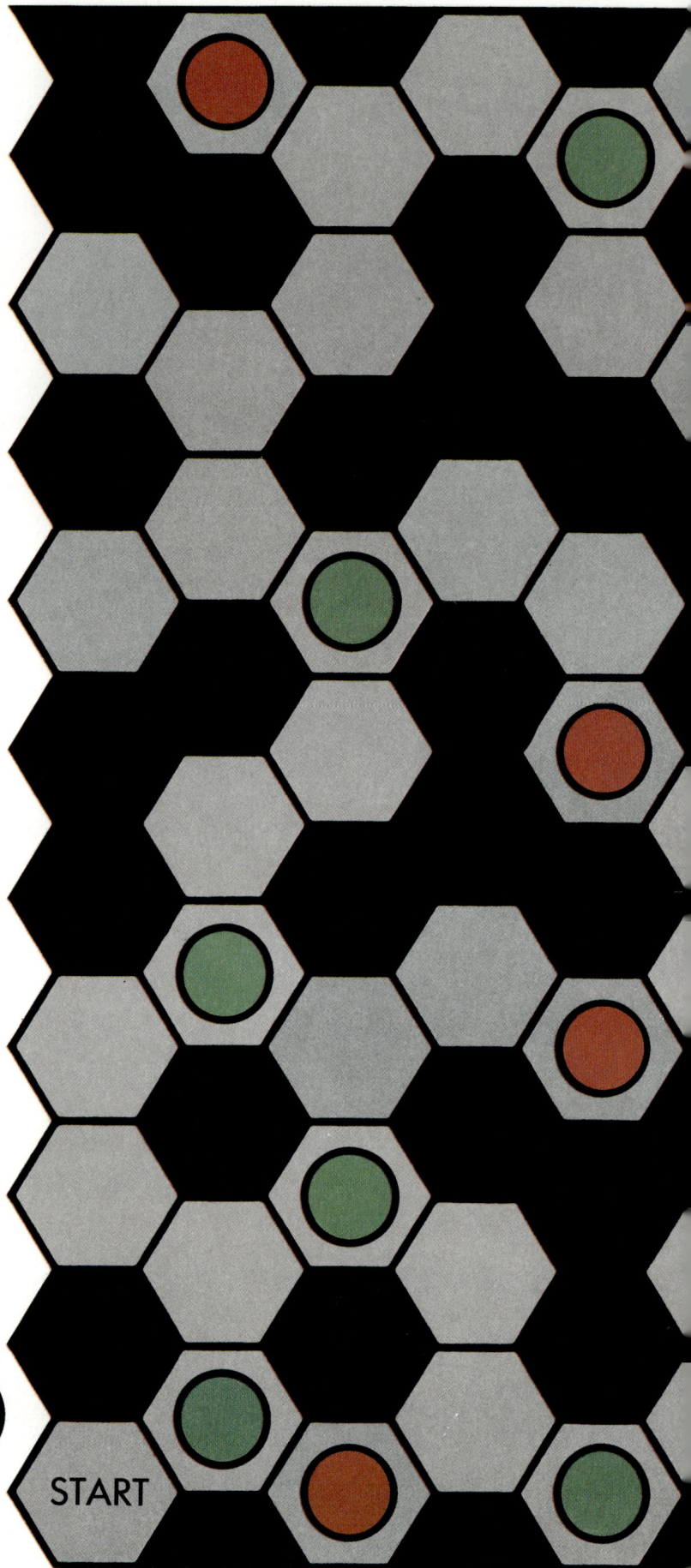

START

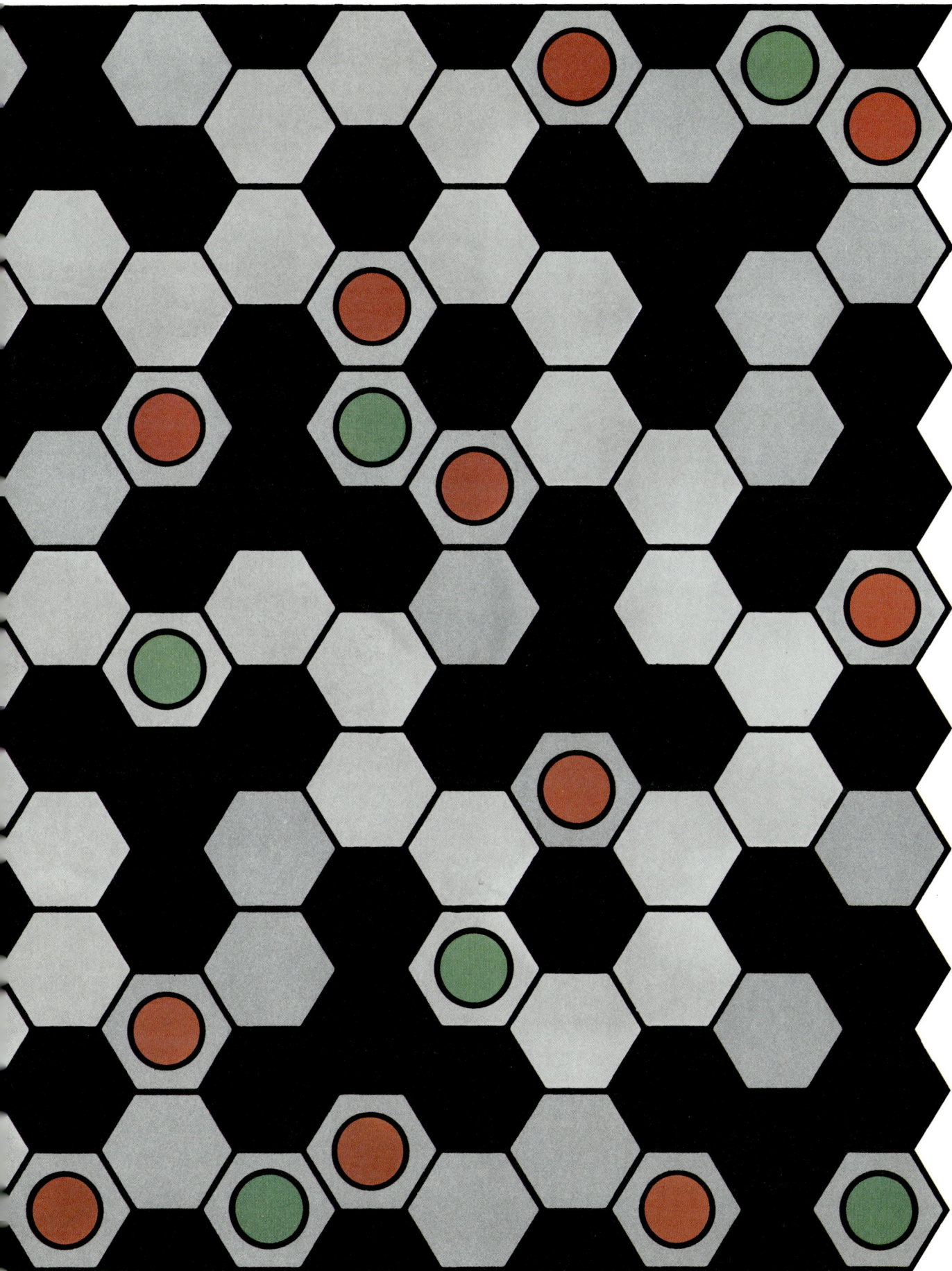

Ludo Trivia

This is a 2 player game. To find out who starts first, throw a dice. The players start at their respective ends of the board. The arrows show direction of play. Player 1 starts by looking at the first of his questions. There are four choices of answer for each of them. If, for instance, the answer is thought to be 'C', then player 1 presses Questron on the first 'C' along the first of the A, B, C, D blocks. If this gives a correct result, he moves to the next question pressing Questron on the letter in the next block which corresponds to the supposed answer.

If this is correct, the player continues. If not, it is player 2's turn, who continues in the same fashion, answering his questions along his part of the board.

When a player has successfully answered his five questions, he moves on to his second arrow. He proceeds to track Questron through the '?' block. If he gets a buzz and red light, he goes back to the arrow, and passes the turn over to the other player. The first player to reach the centre of the board is the winner.

PLAYER ONE

● What is the capital of China?
A. Shanghai **B.** Hong Kong
C. Moscow **D.** Peking

● In what year did Armstrong land on the moon?
A. 1968 **B.** 1969
C. 1970 **D.** 1966

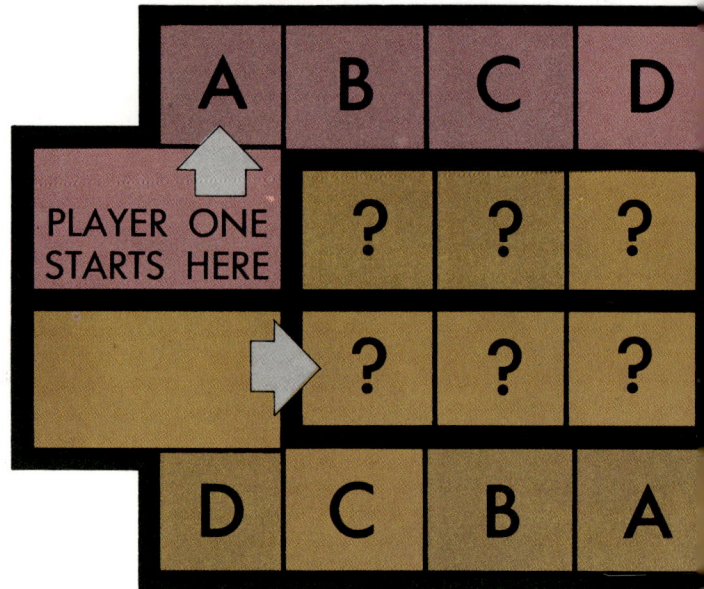

● What is Hollywood famous for?
A. Films **B.** Cars
C. Shops **D.** Fashion

● What is a 'dromedary'?
A. A Fish **B.** A Bird
C. A Camel **D.** An Antelope

● Who wrote the 'water music'?
A. Hinge **B.** Handel
C. Löch **D.** Himmel

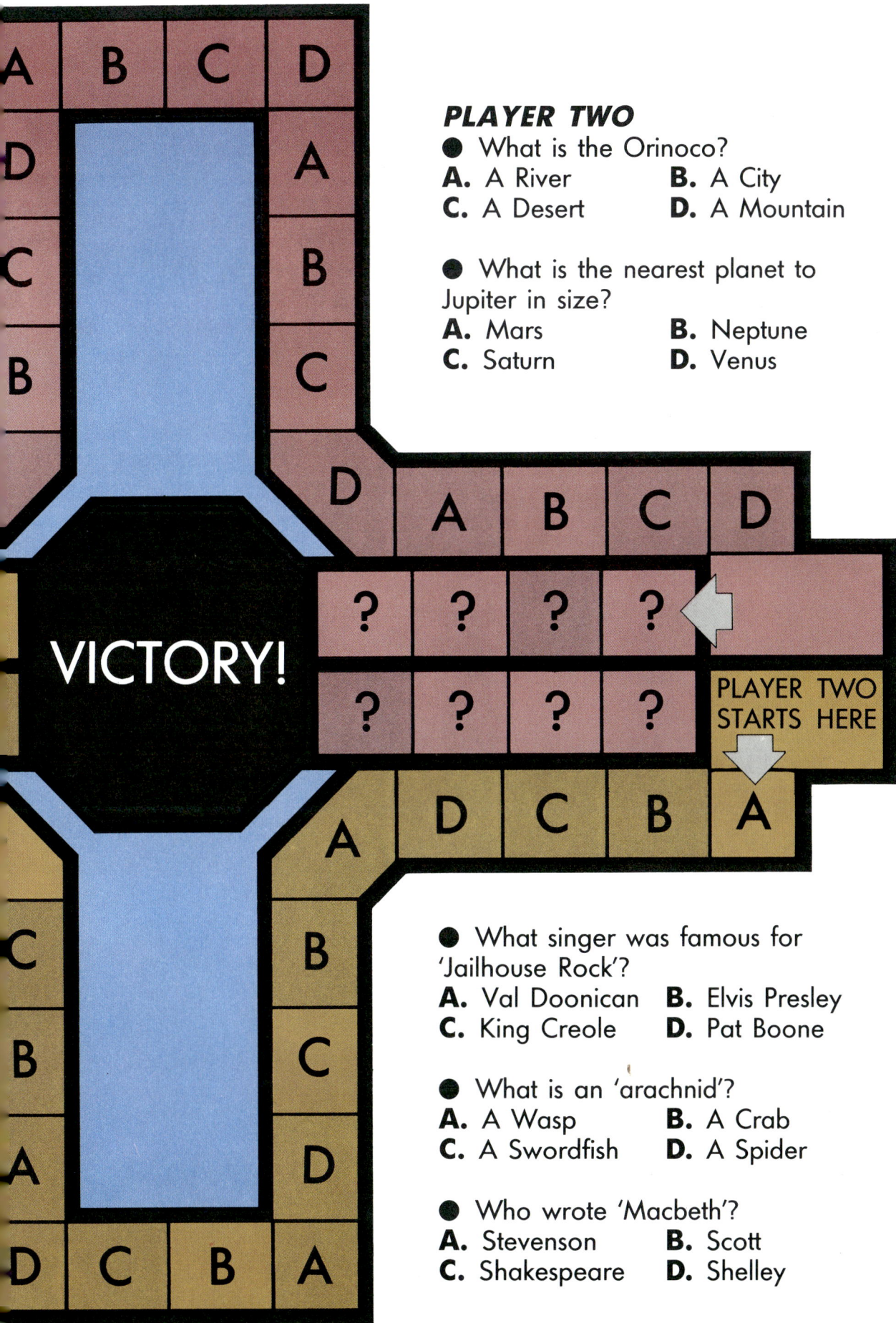

The board layout shows lettered and question-mark spaces (A, B, C, D and ?) forming pathways leading to the center space marked **VICTORY!**

PLAYER TWO STARTS HERE

PLAYER TWO

● What is the Orinoco?
A. A River **B.** A City
C. A Desert **D.** A Mountain

● What is the nearest planet to Jupiter in size?
A. Mars **B.** Neptune
C. Saturn **D.** Venus

● What singer was famous for 'Jailhouse Rock'?
A. Val Doonican **B.** Elvis Presley
C. King Creole **D.** Pat Boone

● What is an 'arachnid'?
A. A Wasp **B.** A Crab
C. A Swordfish **D.** A Spider

● Who wrote 'Macbeth'?
A. Stevenson **B.** Scott
C. Shakespeare **D.** Shelley

Le Mans

This is a game of skill and dexterity. Track Questron around the course, avoiding the other cars and steering clear of hazards. Every time you make a mistake, return to the start.

START

The object of the game is to achieve the fastest time for five complete, consecutive laps.

Jungle Trail

Help Jungle Jim reach his girlfriend June who is being frightened by a ferocious lion!

Use Questron to track his route, first to the lion and then on to June. Beware of the crocodiles and snakes!

START

Air Combat Game

1). Study this view of the sky, from your cockpit. Flying in the middle of a dog fight are enemy planes (the white ones) mixed in with friendly planes (the blue ones). Your aircraft carrier cruises across the horizon. Now cover the page...

2). It is night-time. You have to remember where the enemy planes were. Spot Questron on the squares you think contain them. A 'victory roll' confirms a hit. A normal result means you've hit thin air. A negative result, however, means you've hit a friendly plane — or worse; your aircraft carrier. See how many enemy planes you can hit before making a mistake....

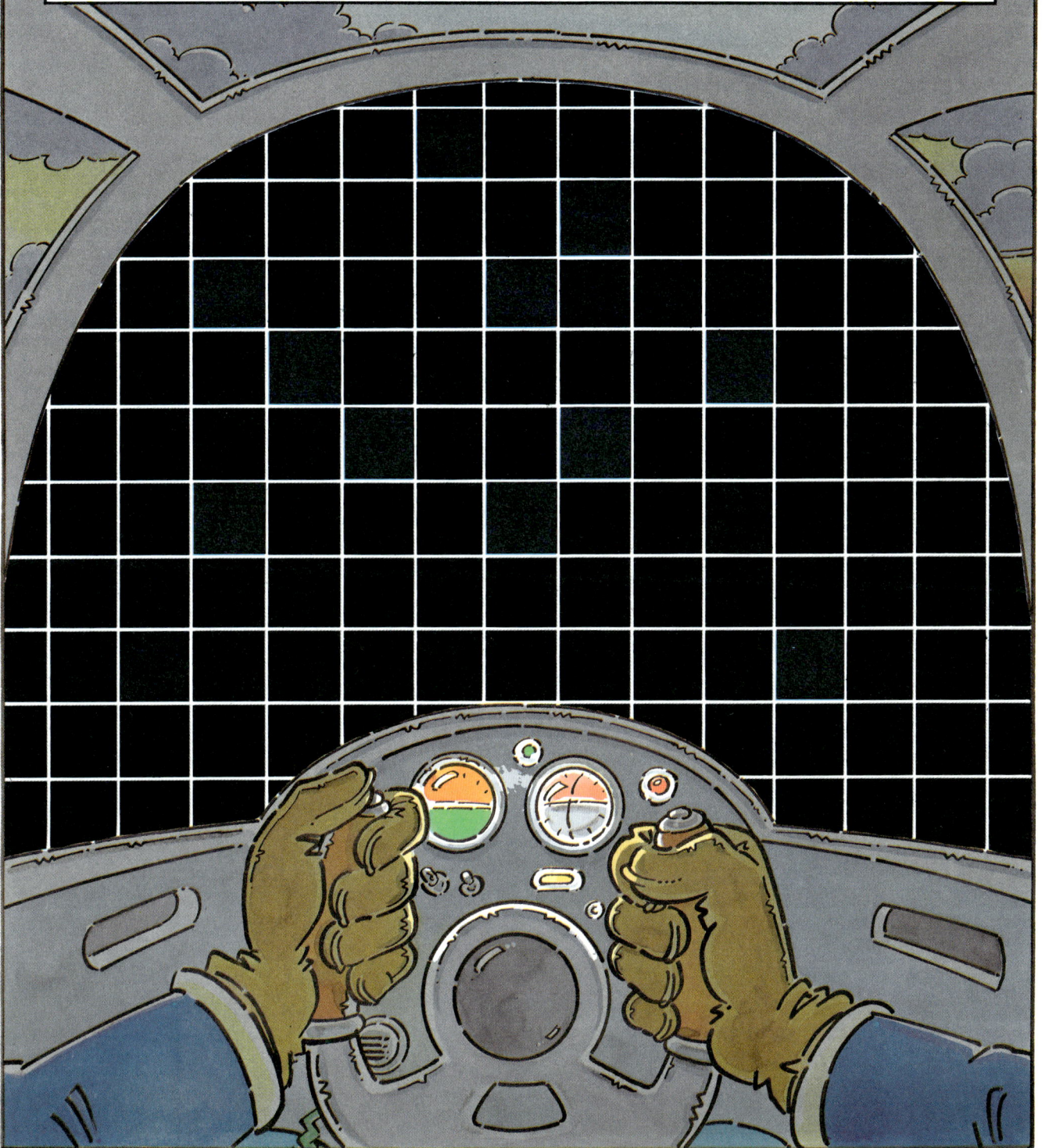

Objects

This is a test of your memory. Study this collection of objects for 15 seconds. There are 21 of them to memorise. Now cover the page . . .

SKY ROC

MATCHES

Spot Questron on the names of the objects you remember seeing on the previous page. They are all here somewhere. When you've worked out which of these 33 objects were on the previous page, go back and spot Questron on the dots next to the objects which are dangerous.

Toothbrush	Green Welly	Dice
Paintpot	Butterfly	Marble
Cup	Book	Comb
Sausage	Sweet	Fork
Knitting	Rocket	Matchbox
Hammer	Plate	Handbag
Hairbrush	Conker	Apple
Penknife	Lemon	Eye Glass
Lightbulb	Thimble	Pencil
Paperclip	Toy Car	Calculator
Vase	Sharpener	Ruler

Questron®

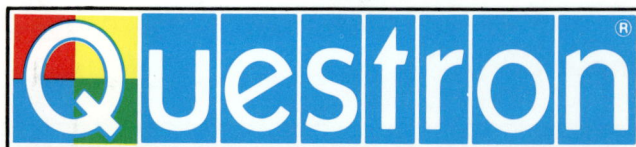

There are three series of Questron titles — Little Q, Early Learner and Explorer — all specifically written to combine learning and fun for a wide range of ages. Early Learner and Explorer books are designed for use with the Questron electronic answer wand. The Little Q titles are used with their very own easy-to-handle Little Q wand (as shown on the inside front cover of this book).

EXPLORER SERIES

AGES 7+

Fact-filled Questron Explorers cover a wonderful range of topics for children to discover and explore. The colourful 32-page books add an extra dimension to favourite subjects and are ideal back-up material for school topic work. A great bonus is the full-colour giant wall poster in all Explorer books.

Titles in the Explorer series

The solar system
Wildlife of the world
Britain's heritage
Peoples of the world
Birds and butterflies
Dinosaur world

LITTLE Q SERIES

AGES 2-5

The bright, colourful titles in the Little Q range help younger children learn the all-important basic skills they will need before starting school. The activities are designed to be repeated to reinforce learning and help children remember. They each contain a super pull-out wall frieze.

Titles in the Little Q series

ABC...
123...
Counting
Very first words
Early skills
Going to the Zoo

SERIF GAMES LIMITED
SERIF HOUSE, HADLEIGH ROAD, IPSWICH, SUFFOLK, IP2 0EE